# THE ADVENTURES OF ROBIN HOOD

OLIVER EMANUEL

# THE ADVENTURES OF
# ROBIN HOOD

OBERON BOOKS
LONDON

WWW.OBERONBOOKS.COM

First published in 2014 by Oberon Books Ltd

521 Caledonian Road, London N7 9RH

Tel: +44 (0) 20 7607 3637 / Fax: +44 (0) 20 7607 3629

e-mail: info@oberonbooks.com

www.oberonbooks.com

PB ISBN: 978-1-78319-120-8

E ISBN: 978-1-78319-619-7

Cover design by James Illman

To VB

## NOTE:

This is a play for two performers in whatever setting you can afford. It could be done with nothing but a matchbox or a huge stack of boxes, trees and party food.

*The Adventures of Robin Hood* was first performed at Eastwood Park Theatre, 7 March 2014 with the following cast:

Billy Mack – ACTOR

Martin McCormick – ACTOR


Douglas Irvine – *Director & Co-designer*

Oliver Emanuel – *Writer*

Suzie Inglis – *Co-designer*

Sergey Jakovsky – *Lighting Designer*

Danny Krass – *Composer/Sound Designer*

Fiona Burness – *Technical & Stage Manager*

Kylie Langford – *Costume Designer*

# 1.

The shadow is moving very slowly across the courtyard.

It's too dark.

That's what gives it away.

Shadows aren't dark. Not really. A shadow is actually made up of different bits of light and dark, a mixture, sort of half and half.

This shadow is totally black.

It creeps along the courtyard and opens the door to the barn.

It's midnight.

There's no moon and everyone in the city of Nottingham is asleep.

Everyone except the Sheriff and his wolf.

The Sheriff is the most hated man in the county.

His best friend is a wolf.

Some folk say that the Sheriff and the wolf were born on the same day and raised by the wolf's mother. No one knows if this is true but they have the same pointed teeth, the same sneer.

Someone has been stealing chickens.

A crime punishable by the loss of an ear.

No one knows who it is.

But tonight the Sheriff has set a trap.

He waits in the darkness with his wolf.

The wolf sniffs the air.

It can smell the armpits of the soldiers lining the walls of
the barn… The delicate scent of the sleeping chickens…
The hot breath of the shadow as it tiptoes towards the
chicken coop…

The soldiers close in.

Each of them carries a flaming torch, hidden beneath a
cloth, ready to reveal the thief at the Sheriff's command.

Three, two, one –

*He clicks his fingers.*

Bright, bright burning light.

ROBIN:          Boo.

A hooded figure, a bag of chickens in one hand and a
bucket of water in the other.

The hooded figure throws the water over the Sheriff,
extinguishing the torch.

SHERIFF:          Stop, thief! After him! Don't let him get
                  away! Get the rascal!

It's mayhem.

Soldiers wave their swords, the Sheriff barks orders and the
wolf tries to eat a stray chicken.

The shadows jump in the torchlight.

SHERIFF:      Where did he go? Did you see him? Grab him!

And there is a thud.

It's just a small thud but everyone hears it.

SHERIFF:      What was that?

The Sheriff marches up to the barn door, dripping wet.

SHERIFF:      Unlock this door. Do you hear? That's an order.

The Sheriff bangs with his fist.

SHERIFF:      How dare you do this to me! Who are you?

And then there is a pause.

And then there is a voice from the behind the barn door.

And the voice says:

ROBIN:        My name is Robin Hood.


# 2.

Hello.

I'm Martin.

And I'm Billy.

Hi.

Welcome.

We're here to tell you a story.

*The Adventures of Robin Hood.*

A story of heroism, of friendship.

Of corruption and murder.

There's a hero and a villain.

Although sometimes it will be difficult to tell which is which.

There are nobles and peasants.

Beggars and thieves.

There are sword fights and archery competitions.

Daring rescues and impossible escapes.

It's a tale that's been told a thousand times.

Although never quite like this.

Set in medieval Britain.

It's about the haves and have nots.

The fat and the hungry.

It's about taking a stand.

And hope.

It's ultimately about hope.

Yes.

It's about the light that shines even in the darkest of places.

Like the new dawn after a dark night.

# 3.

Dawn.

Sherwood Forest.

The word 'forest' actually means an area subject to the King.

To fell a tree or kill a deer is to answer to the law.

But to Robin, the forest is home.

He lives in the canopy of a great oak tree in the centre.

And he is just on his way there now.

He reaches the River Meden, a fast-flowing, tumbling, burbling strip of water that cuts through the forest.

Sometimes Robin swims here or bathes.

Not today.

He wants to get home to breakfast.

There isn't a bridge to cross the river, only a set of stones, fallen loosely across the way.

Robin jumps to the first one then the second then –

He is about to step to the next stone when he senses a looming presence, blocking his path.

A giant.

At least seven foot tall.

Dressed all in green with a staff and an amused expression.

LITTLE JOHN:     What have we got here then, eh?

*The giant snatches the bag.*

ROBIN:           Hey!

LITTLE JOHN:     Chickens?

ROBIN:           Those are mine.

LITTLE JOHN:     Yours?

ROBIN:           Well…sort of. I liberated them from the
                 Sheriff.

LITTLE JOHN:     And now I'm liberating them from you.

Robin could forget the chickens and go back to his tree but
that's not the way he is.

He is brave.

And has a habit of saying stupid things.

ROBIN:           I'll fight you for them.

*The giant laughs.*

LITTLE JOHN:     You? Fight me? Don't be absurd. I would
                 crush you.

ROBIN:           We'll see about that.

And Robin hops back to the riverbank, cuts a birch sapling
with his dagger and marches back to face the giant.

ROBIN:           Are you ready?

LITTLE JOHN:    It's not too late to give up, wee man.

Robin thrusts his staff at the giant's heart but the giant parries it easily. Next Robin swings it at his head but again the giant blocks it. The giant raises his staff to bring it down on Robin's head when Robin stops and points.

ROBIN:          Wait – is that – it's not – is that a *dragon*?

The giant turns his head and Robin smashes his staff down on the giant's toe.

LITTLE JOHN:    Awwww!

Now the fighting becomes fierce.

Where Robin hits out, the giant blocks.

The giant tries to cut Robin down but Robin is smaller and faster and the giant's blows simply beat the air.

LITTLE JOHN:    Give up yet?

ROBIN:          Never!

The two men fight for over an hour, neither one gaining much ground over the other.

*Both breathe heavily.*

ROBIN:          Stop.

LITTLE JOHN:    Stop?

ROBIN:          Stop.

LITTLE JOHN:    I knew you'd give up in the end.

The giant smiles a tired smile but there is something about this smile that angers Robin.

Remember: they are fighting on slippery stones. In the middle of a busy river.

Robin lifts his finger and jabs it into the giant's belly.

The giant wobbles on the stone for a second then tumbles headfirst into the rushing water below.

LITTLE JOHN:    WWWAAAAAAAAAA!

The river swallows the giant and then spits him out.

LITTLE JOHN:    AAAAAAAAHHHHHH!

Robin watches as the current takes hold of the massive man and sets him speeding along, round the bend and over a waterfall.

LITTLE JOHN:    OOOOOOOOOHHHHH!

He clutches at a rock but his fingers can't get a grip.

LITTLE JOHN:    Help me! Help me!

*ROBIN smiles.*

ROBIN:          Can't you swim, big man?

LITTLE JOHN:    No!

The giant vanishes beneath a wave.

He flaps a hand but soon that too is sucked down.

Robin stands on the edge of the bank, watching for bubbles.

Nothing.

ROBIN:          Oh. That's a shame.

*He shakes his head.*

Robin likes to win a fight but not like this.

He never meant to kill the giant.

LITTLE JOHN:   Help…! Help!

Robin doesn't hesitate but dives straight into the icy river.

LITTLE JOHN:   Thank…you…thank you.

ROBIN:   Pleasure.

LITTLE JOHN:   You saved my life.

ROBIN:   Ah well…think nothing of it.

The giant lays a big hand on Robin's shoulder.

LITTLE JOHN:   Could you use a friend?

ROBIN:   What's your name?

LITTLE JOHN:   John Little.

ROBIN:   Little?

LITTE JOHN:   But most folk call me Little John.

ROBIN:   Good to meet you, Little John. I'm Robin Hood.

*They shake hands.*

LITTLE JOHN:   Well Robin Hood. After all that, I'm starving. What about some breakfast?

So off they go to the great oak and have the best breakfast that anyone has ever had.

# 4.

*So is Robin Hood a real person?* Yes and no.

*What does that mean?* He's a legend...a myth.

*Define myth, please.* A story that has been told so many times that it's impossible to tell if it's true anymore.

*When do the stories say he lived?* About a thousand years ago.

*Really?* Yes.

*And what is he?* An outlaw.

*What crime did he commit?* Some people say he killed one of the King's deer. Others that he killed a soldier.

*What's the truth?* Nobody knows.

*Is that why he lives in Sherwood Forest?* Exactly.

*What is Robin Hood like?* He's a brilliant shot with a bow and arrow.

*Is he?* The best in the county.

*What else?* He's great at disguising himself. Oh and he has excellent hair.

*Ha.* What? It's true.

*What are his weaknesses?* Hmmm. He's not very good at sharing. And he often says stupid things that get him into trouble.

*What does Robin Hood do all day?* Hunts. Or thinks up interesting ways to annoy the Sheriff of Nottingham.

*Why doesn't he like the Sheriff?* The Sheriff is a rogue who squeezes the common people for every penny they have.

*Isn't there a king?* The King is away, fighting a war in the Holy Land.

*When is he coming back?* Nobody knows.

*So the Sheriff is in charge?* Yes…for the time being.

*Does Robin Hood fight the Sheriff?* Wait and see

# 5.

Robin and Little John are hungry.

Very hungry.

It's not that they are greedy but they finished the chicken two days ago and haven't eaten since.

To stop their bellies rumbling too loudly, they are playing a game.

| | |
|---|---|
| ROBIN: | If you could eat anything in the world what would it be? |
| LITTLE JOHN: | *(Licking his lips.)* Roast duck with oranges and cabbage and potatoes and thick gravy over it all. |
| ROBIN: | I don't like duck. |
| LITTLE JOHN: | What would you have? |
| ROBIN: | Eagle. |

LITTLE JOHN:     What does eagle taste like?

ROBIN:          A bit like swan.

LITTLE JOHN:     Now you're just being silly…

Robin is about to challenge Little John to a duel when they hear the sound of a carriage coming along the road.

The Great North Way, the main road from London to York, runs through Sherwood Forest.

Anyone wishing to travel through the forest knows there is a chance that they will be met by thieves.

But Robin and Little John are not thieves.

No!

They're simply two very hungry outlaws…out for a stroll… Maybe this lord or lady will be generous enough to give them something to eat…

The carriage appears around the bend and the driver pulls the reigns to stop just in front of them.

Inside is an enormously fat nobleman dressed in blue velvet with a black cap that is set to a slant on his fat head.

He is holding a duck leg in one hand and waves it at Robin.

FAT MAN:        Oi! You!

Robin doesn't like being called 'oi'.

He especially doesn't like overweight posh people calling him 'oi'.

But he is very hungry so smiles his most charming smile.

ROBIN:          Can we help you, sir?

FAT MAN:        Yes you can help me. You can help me by
                wiping that smug grin off your face.

ROBIN:          *(Stops smiling.)...*

FAT MAN:        Is this the road to Nottingham?

This is where Robin should bow his head and point south.

Instead he says something stupid.

ROBIN:          What's it worth?

FAT MAN:        Worth?

ROBIN:          A penny perhaps? Or maybe the rest of that
                fine duck leg? My friend here is particularly
                partial to duck.

The fat nobleman splutters with rage.

FAT MAN:        How dare you talk to me like that! I'll beat
                you for such insolence.

And then it happens.

It happens very quickly.

So quickly that the fat nobleman doesn't really see it.

An arrow.

Straight through the duck leg in the fat nobleman's hand.

FAT MAN:        Please – please don't kill me!

Robin is holding a bow and there is an arrow pointed at
the fat nobleman's heart.

Robin reaches into the carriage and takes the fat purse that hangs from the fat nobleman's belt. And the duck leg for good measure.

ROBIN:              Thank you, kind sir. It is so good of you to help those less fortunate than yourself.

The fat nobleman is about to speak when Robin holds up a finger.

ROBIN:              And Nottingham is that way. I should hurry if I were you, sir. There are rogues and thieves in this forest.

# 6.

Robin Hood and Little John open the fat nobleman's purse.

Inside they discover enough gold to feed a village.

For a year.

BOTH:               Wow…

ROBIN:              What should we do with it all?

Even after they take a few gold coins for themselves there is still far too much.

ROBIN:              We could buy a house. Or a couple of horses. Or a really great pair of trousers.

Robin Hood has always had an active imagination.

*LITTLE JOHN shakes his head.*

LITTLE JOHN:     I know what we should do.

                Follow me…


# 7.


We forgot a bit of the story.

We forgot the bit about why Little John is living in the forest.

Most people assume he deserted from the King's army or that he killed a man in a tavern brawl.

It's not true.

This is Little John's story.

LITTLE JOHN:     My dad was the blacksmith in our village.
                It was a good business. Harvests fail and
                animals die, said my dad, but folk will always
                need a blacksmith. But then one day the
                harvest did fail and all of the animals in the
                village died of starvation. The King had
                just gone off on his crusade and the Sheriff
                increased taxes. My dad's business failed,
                he lost his home and Mum went off with
                another man. I could've helped him but I
                was ashamed. He became a drunk and a
                layabout. I left the village to make my own
                way in the world. Then one day I heard he
                had filled his pockets with stones and walked
                into the river. When I found his body, I
                barely recognised the happy and contented
                man who had brought me up. Poverty had
                turned his skin grey, his cheeks hollow.

As Little John finishes, they arrive at the edge of a village to the north of the forest.

It is dusk and the sun has almost set on the dozen or so small cottages that line the road.

ROBIN:          Where are we?

LITTLE JOHN:    Home.

Little John wipes a tear from his eye before taking the purse of gold from Robin.

ROBIN:          Hey! What are you doing? That's mine.

LITTLE JOHN:    Yours?

ROBIN:          Ours.

LITTLE JOHN:    We can't use it all, Robin.

ROBIN:          But – but –

LITTLE JOHN:    Isn't it better to share it with those who need it most…?

Robin has never been very good at sharing.

He's never had very much to share.

ROBIN:          *(Nods.)* Go ahead.

Little John walks along the high street, placing a single gold coin on each doorstep.

When they get to the end of the village, they still have half the gold left.

So they go on to the next village and the village after that too, leaving a small gift of gold to the poor folk of Nottingham.

An old man comes out of his house.

He cries for joy and asks them what kind of lords they are to give away such a fortune.

By the next morning the names of Little John and Robin Hood are legend across the county.

# 8.

Meanwhile…

In Nottingham Castle.

Nottingham is one of the greatest and grandest castles in the kingdom.

Built in the time of William the Conqueror.

And whilst the King is away, fighting his war in the Holy Land, it is in the stewardship of the Sheriff.

He loves the castle.

Every inch of it.

The great hall, the courtyard, the one hundred and thirty-seven bedrooms.

And, of course, the dungeons.

Which are rather full at the moment. What with all these poor folk not paying their taxes and everything. The Sheriff is seriously thinking about an extension...

The Sheriff knows that the castle doesn't actually belong to him but the King has been away that long he often imagines that it does.

His favourite thing is to sit and eat breakfast in the north tower and look out over the city, towards the forest.

But this morning, the Sheriff's breakfast was rudely interrupted by a gang of nobles.

They were complaining about a hooded man and his giant friend who had apparently robbed them on the Great North Way.

One of them had even introduced himself...

SHERIFF: Robin Hood...that name again.

The Sheriff's wolf sits and growls at his feet.

WOLF: Grrr.

SHERIFF: While the King is away, I am the law. It is my duty to protect his property and his nobles. God knows I try to be fair but if word ever reached His Majesty that I let a thief go freely about the forest, I would be for the chop.

Robin Hood must be stopped.

WOLF: Grrr.

SHERIFF: Yes I agree.

I'll put a bounty on his head. Is £20 enough
do you think?

WOLF:            Grrr?

SHERIFF:        No you're right. £10 is fine. No point wasting
                good money, is there? I need a quill.

*He finds a quill and writes on a piece of paper.*

SHERIFF:        That should do it.

*He holds it up.*

SHERIFF:        ROBIN HOOD: WANTED DEAD OR
                ALIVE.


# 9.

Hang on.

What?

Is there something we're missing?

Erm…

The Merry Men.

Of course! How could we forget? It wouldn't be Robin
Hood without the Merry Men, would it?

Absolutely not.

As Robin's fame spreads across the land, he and Little John
are joined by others.

There's Much the Millar's Son.

A youth with a quick temper and even quicker fingers.

And Will Scarlet.

A pretty lad who accidentally killed the husband of one of his numerous lovers.

And Allan A Dale.

A minstrel who wrote a rude song about the Sheriff and had his little fingers chopped off.

Ouch!

And lastly there is Friar Tuck. How do we describe Friar Tuck?

Erm…

This is Friar Tuck.

*FRIAR TUCK enters, holding a beer.*

*FRIAR TUCK sings* Everything I Do *by Bryan Adams.*

The most honest man you will ever meet. Or the rudest. Sometimes it's difficult to tell whether he is being extremely honest or extremely rude. Friar Tuck spends most of his days drinking and shouting at God.

*He continues to sing.*

*He falls over.*

Don't worry. God doesn't pay too much attention.

These are all wanted men, criminals and outlaws.

Yet to Robin they are the best friends in the world.

He calls them his 'Merry Men'.

Together they rob from the rich and give to the poor and they are so good at it that someone writes a song about them.

Not a very good song.

No, not a very good song.

The code of the Merry Men is very simple.

1. Always be polite.

2. Never take more than a person can afford.

3. Don't kill anyone. Not unless you absolutely have to.

And so it isn't long before Robin Hood is so famous and loved by the poor folk of Nottingham that he is known as the 'King of the forest'.

# 10.

SHERIFF:     King of the forest?

Is this a joke?

I wanted Robin Hood hanging from the nearest tree by now. I wanted his heart cut out with a spoon.

What is wrong with everyone?

*He kicks the wolf.*

WOLF:     Ow ow!

SHERIFF:    A thief. Nothing but a common thief. And
            the people love him. How does that happen?

WOLF:       Grrr…

SHERIFF:    No one understands what it's like being a
            sheriff. The long hours. The pressure.

*He brandishes a letter.*

SHERIFF:    See this? Another letter from the King,
            demanding money for his war. What am I
            to do? I send as much as I can but the more
            successful I am at gathering taxes, the more
            the King expects. It's very hard.

WOLF:       Grrr grrr.

SHERIFF:    Thank you. I appreciate it.

*He shakes his head.*

SHERIFF:    I need a new plan. If the people won't bring
            me Robin Hood then *logically* I need Robin
            Hood to bring himself to me.

            So…how do you trap a wolf?

WOLF:       Grrr?

SHERIFF:    No I know you wouldn't but hypothetically.

WOLF:       Grrr.

SHERIFF:    Yes exactly. You put out bait. You put out
            bait and set a trap. Then you wait for the
            wolf to walk straight in.

            All I have to do is think of the right kind of
            bait for Robin Hood…

*He thinks…*

# 11.

*ROBIN and LITTLE JOHN are walking through the forest.*

LITTLE JOHN:     An archery competition, Robin?

ROBIN:     That's what I heard, Little John.

LITTLE JOHN:     What's the prize?

ROBIN:     A golden arrow.

LITTLE JOHN:     Wow.

ROBIN:     Brilliant, eh?

LITTLE JOHN:     Yeah brilliant…but you know it's a trap.

*ROBIN gives him a look.*

ROBIN:     What are you talking about?

LITTLE JOHN:     Well… The Sheriff is your enemy isn't he?

ROBIN:     Definitely.

LITTLE JOHN:     And what is Robin Hood famous for?

ROBIN:     Being a hero of the people.

LITTLE JOHN:     What else?

ROBIN:     Having excellent hair.

LITTLE JOHN:     And…?

ROBIN:     And being the greatest archer in the county.

LITTLE JOHN:     Exactly.

ROBIN:          So?

LITTLE JOHN:    So if I wanted to trap the greatest archer in
                the county, what better way to lure him in
                than an archery competition?

ROBIN:          Ah.

LITTLE JOHN:    Yes?

ROBIN:          I see your point.

*Slight pause.*

ROBIN:          But I must have that golden arrow!

LITTLE JOHN:    The Sheriff will kill you.

ROBIN:          So what?

LITTLE JOHN:    Robin.

ROBIN:          I'm not thinking of myself, Little John. How
                much do you think a solid gold arrow is
                worth? Hundreds. We could feed the whole
                county for a month.

LITTLE JOHN:    You would risk your life to enter a stupid
                archery competition?

ROBIN:          I'm not afraid of the Sheriff.

LITTLE JOHN:    Well you should be.

*ROBIN stops.*

ROBIN:          Hang on. I've got an idea.

LITTLE JOHN:    What?

ROBIN: You're absolutely right, Little John. I can't enter the archery competition.

LITTLE JOHN: Phew…

ROBIN: To be precise, Robin Hood can't enter…but I can.

LITTLE JOHN: Eh?

ROBIN: Come on, let's go. *(He turns around.)* We haven't got all day. I'll explain the plan on the way.

LITTLE JOHN: Where are we going, Robin?

ROBIN: Isn't it obvious?

We are going to buy a hat.

# 12.

– Welcome back, ladies and gentlemen, to a meadow outside the great city of Nottingham. We're here for the big event. Yes it's the First Annual Nottinghamshire Archery Competition. It's a beautiful day isn't it, Brian?

– Yes, Brian, it's a beautiful day.

– Perfect weather. Barely a cloud in the sky. Excitement is high. For those just joining us, what have we seen so far?

– We've had the heats, the quarters and the semis. Next up, the final!

– Who's in the running?

– The Sheriff's Sergeant-At-Arms was the favourite coming into today's competition.

– But there's a hotshot contender coming up from behind isn't there, Brian?

– Are you referring to the Frenchman?

– Yes indeed the Frenchman or, as they say in France, *Le Francais*.

– *Mais oui!*

– What do we know about this mysterious character?

– Very little, Brian. As you can see, the Frenchman wears a very large hat so we can't even see his face.

– Bizarre. But the Frenchman has certainly made his mark.

– Absolutely. The Sheriff's Sergeant is looking a bit uncomfortable.

– The Sheriff's not looking too happy either.

– No, Brian. He's got a scowl on him that would frighten a badger. There's a heavy military presence here today. The Sheriff's men line the meadow. The official word is that it's for the security of the crowd but I heard a whisper that the Sheriff was hoping to catch Robin Hood today but the local boy has yet to show his face and –

– I'll have to interrupt you there, Brian, because here they come. The final is about to begin. First up, the Sheriff's Sergeant. The Sergeant says that if he wins today, he will dedicate the golden arrow to his boss the Sheriff. Right here we go. The waiting is over…

*The Sergeant raises his bow.*

*He shoots.*

GOLD!

– Amazing, Brian! Perfect 20! The Sergeant is smiling. It couldn't have gone better, could it Brian?

– No it really couldn't.

– Is it all over for the Frenchman?

– I don't know, Brian. Or as they say in France, *je ne sais pas.*

– Here he comes…

*The Frenchman raises his bow.*

*He shoots.*

CRACK!

– I – I don't believe it – the Frenchman's arrow has split the Sergeant's arrow down the middle! I've never seen anything like it. There are people on the pitch. They think it's all over.

– It is now!

– The Frenchman has won!

– The Sergeant shakes his head in disappointment. The Frenchman is jubilant. The crowd is cheering and yelling.

– The Sheriff goes over to present the golden arrow.

– Wait. I think if we lean in close, we will hear a few words from the Sheriff…

*SHERIFF hands over the golden arrow.*

SHERIFF:        Well played, *Monsieur*. Very well done.

ROBIN:          *Merci beaucoup*, Sheriff.

SHERIFF:        You shot even better than Robin Hood.

ROBIN:          Who's 'dat?

SHERIFF:        I could've sworn the archery competition
                would have drawn the rogue out of hiding.

ROBIN:          Perhaps 'e guessed your 'ittle trick.

SHERIFF:        Impossible.

ROBIN:          Well, I 'ear he is very clever...

SHERIFF:        Hmmm. You seem very familiar to me,
                *Monsieur*. Have we met before?

ROBIN:          *Oh non, non.* I'm sure I would remember if I
                'ad 'ad the honour...

SHERIFF:        Well anyway...well done.

– The Sheriff's obviously not happy with the result but
today was a game of two halves wasn't it, Brian?

– It certainly was.

– Now we see the Frenchman join his friends and leave the
meadow, the golden arrow held aloft in victory. He raises
his hat to the crowd and we see his face at last –

– No it can't be – it's – it's Robin Hood!

– The Frenchman is none other than the champion of the
common man, Robin Hood!

– Brilliant!

– The Sheriff's soldiers are after him at once but I don't think they will catch up –

– Robin Hood is almost at the edge of the forest –

– The soldier's close in but –

– OOO –

– That was close –

– Robin Hood has gotten away…

– What an end to the day. I didn't see that coming. And by the look on the Sheriff's face, neither did he! What a turn of events.

# 13.

However the next morning, the good people of Nottingham awake to find a proclamation nailed to the door of the castle.

It says:

SHERIFF:    By order of the Sheriff and in the name of the King, every man, woman and child over the age of eight is ordered to pay a tax to fund the security of the county. Any person not paying this tax will be liable to prosecution. Further, all forms of begging – including that of players – is outlawed on pain of death.

What the – ?

Taxes are already high.

Most folk barely have enough to keep a roof over their head.

This will make it impossible.

And as the folk of Nottingham are taking in this disastrous news, a squad of the Sheriff's guard slip out of the gates unseen and head towards Sherwood Forest…

# 14.

Robin is surrounded.

A hundred men.

No, not just men.

Women too.

And children.

Lean and bony, faces bright with sweat and dirt.

Robin stands in the middle of a clearing in the forest, totally outnumbered.

This is the end.

He's always known he would die but he didn't imagine it would be today…

The sun is bright and high in the sky.

And then a woman speaks.

Bold and fearless from the middle of the crowd.

| MARION: | Are you Robin Hood? |
|---|---|
| ROBIN: | What – what do you want with him? |
| MARION: | Please answer the question, sir. We have come a long way and are tired and hungry. |

Robin blinks.

At first he thought they were carrying swords and spears but now he looks closer, it's only bundles of rags and old sticks of furniture.

*He laughs.*

| MARION: | What's so funny? |
|---|---|
| ROBIN: | I thought you were sent by the Sheriff to kill me. |
| MARION: | The Sheriff has raised taxes again. We are starving. We have been thrown out of our homes. We have nothing. |
| ROBIN: | What has that to do with me? |
| MARION: | Everyone knows that Robin Hood fights the Sheriff. We have come to join you. |
| ROBIN: | Join me? |
| MARION: | Yes. |

*He bursts out laughing again.*

| ROBIN: | You crack me up. |
|---|---|
| MARION: | This isn't a joke. |
| ROBIN: | Of course it is. And it's a good one. |

| | |
|---|---|
| MARION: | We want to fight. |
| ROBIN: | Fight? |
| MARION: | The Sheriff must be stopped. |
| ROBIN: | And you're going to stop him? |
| MARION: | Yes. |
| ROBIN: | But you're just a bunch of useless peasants. What can you do against the Sheriff's trained men? |
| MARION: | Please help us. |
| ROBIN: | Don't be stupid. Go home. |

Robin is about to go off back to the great oak when the woman steps out from the crowd.

Now you might not think she is beautiful.

Maybe to most folk she isn't.

Robin has never been very good with beautiful women.

It's their lips… Or their eyes… Or their…something.

Makes his head hurt.

And this woman…standing in front of him…with the forest light just so…

He opens his mouth to speak and –

She punches him in the face.

*ROBIN stumbles.*

ROBIN:          Aw. What was that for?

MARION:         Idiot.

ROBIN:          Me?

MARION:         I could kill you.

ROBIN:          That really hurt.

*She puts a dagger to his throat.*

*He stares at her.*

ROBIN:          Who are you?

This is the first sensible question Robin has asked.

Her name is Marion.

And this is Marion's story:

MARION:         My father died when I was a baby. He was a
                squire. Not a rich one, with just a farm and a
                few fields. My mother didn't want to marry
                again so we worked the land ourselves. It
                wasn't much of a life but it was our own. And
                then the Sheriff told us that our land was
                needed for the King's crops and we would
                have to sell it. He offered an outrageous
                price and my mother refused. She was set
                upon in the night. Beaten almost to death.
                The next day, the Sheriff offered an even
                lower price and my mother was too scared to
                say no. This is happening all over. Folk are
                being turned out of their homes by nobles
                with money and the might to keep the prices
                low.

*Slight pause.*

| MARION: | This isn't a game, Robin Hood. It might have been to you before but not now. The Sheriff and those like him want it all. If we are to stand any kind of chance, we need to fight back. |
| ROBIN: | But – but we have no weapons. |
| MARION: | Here are blacksmiths and fletchers, all the craftsmen we could ever need. |
| ROBIN: | You are not soldiers. |
| MARION: | Teach us. You and your Merry Men together. |
| ROBIN: | But – |
| MARION: | But? |
| ROBIN: | But what if I don't know what to do? |
| MARION: | Ask. |
| | You're not alone anymore. |

# 15.

It's the Sheriff's birthday.

His favourite day of the year.

All the nobles from far and wide are invited to a special feast and the Sheriff gets to boast about how many taxes he has squeezed from the people.

Oh and if they get bored, they might hang a peasant or two.

It's tremendous fun.

The great hall has been decorated.

Great mountains of food and a lake of wine.

The wolf has a bow around its neck.

Everything is perfect.

SHERIFF:        Let's get this party started!

*The SHERIFF dances.*

The Sheriff is drunk.

SHERIFF:        No I'm not. Who said that? Off with your
                head!

Well, he's a little bit drunk.

He's drunk enough that he starts telling anyone who will
listen about how brilliant he is.

SHERIFF:        Don't you see? There's no one in the county
                to touch me. I collect more taxes than
                anyone.

                I'm the best.

It's always the same at the Sheriff's birthday.

The only thing to do is nod and smile and stuff as much
party food into your pockets as you can.

But then someone asks a question.

GUEST:          What about Robin Hood?

*Music stops.*

The Sheriff can't make out the face of the questioner.

SHERIFF:  Robin Hood? Pah. Not scared of him. Didn't even show up for the archery competition and he's meant to be the greatest archer around. Whatever. I'll tell you what Robin Hood is…he's a coward.

An arrow.

Cuts through the hubbub and the jollity and imbeds itself at the Sheriff's feet.

He is suddenly sober.

SHERIFF:  Who did that?

A shadow.

Too dark and too quick.

Flits through the crowd and out of the door.

SHERIFF:  There! There! After him!

The guests choke on their food, the soldiers grab their swords and the Sheriff chases after the shadow.

Along corridors, down staircases and out into the courtyard.

He spots the shadow running over to the gate.

SHERIFF:  Stop!

And to his surprise, the shadow does exactly that.

The shadow stops, turns and smiles.

ROBIN:        Happy birthday, Sheriff. I'm sorry but I
              forgot to get you a present.

SHERIFF:      Ha! Your neck in a noose will be gift enough
              for me, Robin Hood.

ROBIN:        Not this time.

SHERIFF:      Eh?

And that is when the moon comes out from behind a cloud
and the Sheriff sees them all for the first time.

Men and women and children.

Lining the battlements.

Each a bow and an arrow pointed straight at the Sheriff.

SHERIFF:      What – what is this?

ROBIN:        These are my Merry Men. And Women. My
              Merry People.

SHERIFF:      What do they want?

ROBIN:        Don't you feel bad that while the poorest of
              the county starve you and your friends stuff
              their faces?

SHERIFF:      I – I'm sorry?

ROBIN:        Then you won't mind if we take our fair
              share will you?

Before the Sheriff can think of something to say, ten or so
children disappear into the castle to emerge a few moments
later with bundles of fine food and wine.

They go back and forth until the Sheriff's banquet has completely gone.

*ROBIN eats something.*

ROBIN:          Oh. What is this? Hmmm. Tastes a bit like frog.

*He wipes his hands on the SHERIFF's shirt.*

ROBIN:          Thanks so much, Sheriff. Yum yum. That was delicious. And again many happy returns.

Robin clicks his fingers and as if by magic the Merry People disappear into the dark night.

The Sheriff stamps his foot and shouts.

SHERIFF:        This…means…war.


# 16.


ROBIN:          Did you see his face, Marion?

MARION:         I did, Robin.

ROBIN:          Wasn't it brilliant?

MARION:         Brilliant.

ROBIN:          The way the arrow almost hit his foot. Everyone stopped talking and the terrified look in his face it was…it was brilliant.

MARION:         Yeah…

It is late.

Everyone else is asleep, exhausted after the Sheriff's party.

Robin and Marion have become firm friends.

At least, Robin hopes they have.

It's sometimes difficult to tell whether Marion likes him or just finds him annoying.

He can be quite annoying.

ROBIN:          Just one more thing –

MARION:          Shut up now, Robin. Sleep well.

But he doesn't.

Robin lies awake and looks up at the sky as it changes from black to purple to blue.

Everything has changed in a few short months.

Before he was just a thief but now after months of sword practice and archery lessons, he is the leader of an army of the people.

It's amazing.

He can hardly believe it's real.

The sky has turned misty and grey and thick and –

Wait a second –

# 17.

Is that…fire?

Yes.

Yes that's definitely fire.

Robin stands in the canopy of the great oak and looks all around.

Trees and bushes and grass, all burning.

It's everywhere.

He grabs up his horn.

*Blows his horn.*

ROBIN:              FIRE!

*LITTLE JOHN appears.*

LITTLE JOHN:    What is it, Robin?

ROBIN:              Fire, Little John.

LIITLE JOHN:    Where?

ROBIN:              Look.

LITTLE JOHN:    Oh no. How did this happen?

ROBIN:              The Sheriff.

LITTLE JOHN:    He wouldn't.

ROBIN:              Oh no?

LITTLE JOHN:    What do we do?

ROBIN:              We have to get everyone out, Little John.

There's panic.

Children screaming, adults yelling at each other.

The fire snakes in and out of the trees. It's getting difficult to breathe. The smoke is blinding.

Robin grabs Little John and the other Merry Men.

ROBIN: We must get as many weapons as we can. Everything you can carry. The Sheriff will be waiting for us on the other side of the fire. Ready? Then let's go.

They snatch up bows and arrows and swords and spears and shields.

But there isn't a single break in the fire and it's closing in fast.

LITTLE JOHN: What do we do, Robin?

ROBIN: I don't know, Little John.

LITTLE JOHN: We need a plan.

ROBIN: Give me a minute.

LITTLE JOHN: Don't think we have a minute, Robin. It's getting awfully warm around here.

*ROBIN snaps his fingers.*

ROBIN: A bath! We need to take a bath, Little John.

LITTLE JOHN: What the – ?

ROBIN: Listen. If we get ourselves completely soaked we will be protected from the fire. We'll able to run right through it.

LITTLE JOHN: Run through the fire? Are you crazy?

ROBIN: Probably.

But there isn't a better plan so the Merry Men grab the buckets of washing water that sit beneath each tree and pour it over their heads.

LITTLE JOHN: Aw that's cold.

ROBIN: Are you ready, Little John?

LITTLE JOHN: As I'll ever be, Robin.

ROBIN: Right then. Here goes...

And so they charge at the burning wall of fire.

BOTH: AAAAAAHHHHHHH!

# 18.

*A dungeon.*

*Night.*

*The sound of dripping.*

*ROBIN in chains, alone.*

*Silence.*

*The SHERIFF enters, eating an apple.*

ROBIN: What did you do?

SHERIFF: Me?

ROBIN: The fire.

SHERIFF:     Oh.

             Yes.

ROBIN:       How could you?

SHERIFF:     Easy enough…a flame here and there…
             nature took care of the rest.

ROBIN:       There were children in there –

SHERIFF:     Children you trained to kill.

ROBIN:       Did they get out?

SHERIFF:     Some of them.

ROBIN:       I'll kill you.

*He strains against the chains but the SHERIFF is just out of reach.*

SHERIFF:     You can't blame me for this, Robin Hood. It
             was you that got them killed.

ROBIN:       That's a lie.

SHERIFF:     Your arrogance and your vanity.

ROBIN:       What are you talking about?

SHERIFF:     Why did you promise them that you would
             lead them to victory? Were you so hungry
             for fame?

ROBIN:       That's not fair.

SHERIFF:     Isn't it? You set yourself up as the hero of
             the people but do you have any idea what it
             takes to be a real leader? To make decisions

|  | – sometimes difficult, tough decisions – for the good not just yourself but of everyone. |
|---|---|
| ROBIN: | That's not how it is. |
| SHERIFF: | You don't do you? |
| ROBIN: | Shut up. |
| SHERIFF: | You're only in it for your own glory, Robin Hood. You don't really care about anyone else, do you? I know what you think of me but I believe you are the monster here. |

*Silence.*

| ROBIN: | What happens now? |
|---|---|
| SHERIFF: | Now you say your prayers and wait for tomorrow. |
| ROBIN: | Tomorrow? |
| SHERIFF: | Tomorrow you will die. |

*He chucks the apple core and exits.*

# 19.

Robin tries to sleep that night but he can't.

It's not the rats or the spiders in the dungeons or the thought of being hanged in the morning.

No.

It's the faces.

Little John's face. Marion, Much, Will Scarlet, Allan A Dale, Friar Tuck and all the rest.

When Robin closes his eyes he can see them right here as if they are standing in front of him.

He's let them down.

He's failed.

The dawn is a long time coming and even though he stands on tiptoes he still can't see the forest through the bars.

## 20.

The courtyard again.

Bright morning sunshine.

Robin is lead through the crowd towards the scaffold.

This.

Is.

It.

There are lots of people. Not just from the city, from the villages too. Everyone come to see the hanging of famous Robin Hood.

Soldiers and the Sheriff's men line the walls.

He scans the crowd, looking for a face he recognises.

No one.

Twelve steps up to the scaffold and the knotted rope.

His legs feel heavy.

The executioner – a massive and brutal man from London who has come up specially – is dressed all in black with a black hood over his face, pushes Robin roughly.

EXECUTIONER:  Get along there! Move it!

The air is surprisingly clear when he reaches the top… Robin could almost imagine he was back by the river… He breathes deeply and closes his eyes…

This is it.

EXECUTIONER:  Does the condemned man have any final
                        words?

Robin could say something.

Something heroic and noble.

But he would probably muck it up and end up saying something stupid.

ROBIN:            No…nothing.

The executioner holds the end of the rope.

This is it.

And then to Robin's surprise, the executioner says something in his ear:

EXECUTIONER:  When I count to three, jump.

ROBIN:            Eh?

EXECUTIONER:  Just do it, Robin.

ROBIN:          Little John?

EXECUTIONER:  Ssshh.

Robin does everything he can, not to laugh.

EXECUTIONER:  Three, two...one.

And Robin jumps.

And the scaffold explodes.

A massive bang like an earthquake or the end of the world rocks the whole castle.

The Sheriff can't believe his eyes.

It was there one second and the next –

BANG!

Another explosion.

This time the courtyard walls collapse.

Gunpowder.

Somehow the Merry Men must have raided the King's armoury and got hold of barrels of gunpowder.

But how?

BANG!

BANG!

BANG!

The north tower, the entrance hall, the chapel.

What is happening?

The Sheriff's precious castle is coming down before his eyes and there's nothing he can do.

SHERIFF:        No no no.

His soldiers are running this way and that but they don't know what to do.

People are screaming.

The Sheriff scans the crowd but there is no sign of Robin Hood.

It's like looking for a needle in a big stack of needles.

SHERIFF:        RRRRAAAAAAAA!


# 21.


Meanwhile…

Safe and hidden beneath an upturned cart, Robin greets his Merry Men.

ROBIN:          What happened, Little John? How did you get into the castle? Have you got many folk with you?

LITTLE JOHN:   We don't have time for questions, Robin. We have to get out of here.

*LITTLE JOHN is about to run but ROBIN shakes his head.*

ROBIN:          No.

LITTLE JOHN:     No?

ROBIN:           No I have to find the Sheriff.

LITTLE JOHN:     And do what?

ROBIN:           End this.

LITTLE JOHN:     We need to get away now.

ROBIN:           If I don't then this will just keep happening
                 over and over again. I need to finish it.

FRIAR TUCK:      But Robin –

    This is Friar Tuck now.

FRIAR TUCK:      But Robin you can't go in there alone.

ROBIN:           I have to.

FRIAR TUCK:      Let us go with you.

ROBIN:           Thanks, Tuck, but I need to face the Sheriff
                 by myself.

FRIAR TUCK:      Why?

ROBIN:           It's… complicated.

MARION:          But Robin –

    This is Marion speaking.

MARION:          But Robin what about the people?

ROBIN:           The people?

MARION:          They need you.

ROBIN:            No I've let them down. I have to make it
                  right.

MARION:           But without a leader, what will they do?

ROBIN:            You can lead them, Marion.

MARION:           What?

ROBIN:            I'm no good to them. You'd be brilliant.

WILL SCARLET:  But Robin –

This is Will Scarlet.

But Robin has had enough.

ROBIN:            Look, Will. Whatever you have to say, could
                  you possibly hold on to your question for a
                  moment?

Will Scarlet nods, Marion blows him a kiss, Little John
hands him his sword and Friar Tuck crosses himself.

ROBIN:            I'll see you later.


# 22.

He finds the Sheriff in the great hall, loading bags full of
gold.

ROBIN:            Off on holiday, Sheriff?

SHERIFF:          Erm…no.

ROBIN:            No?

SHERIFF:          Nothing could be further from my mind.

There are still explosions outside, people yelling. It's a riot.

ROBIN:            It's just you and me, Sheriff.

SHERIFF:          I – I don't want a fight, Robin.

ROBIN:            I'm sure you don't.

SHERIFF:          I'll just take these bags of gold and be off…

ROBIN:            Sounds like a plan.

SHERIFF:          Great.

ROBIN:            But I have a better one. What if I just kill you
                  now and we give all the money back to the
                  people?

SHERIFF:          Ah.

ROBIN:            Yes I may not be perfect but at least I don't
                  steal from ordinary, honest people.

Robin pulls out his sword.

The Sheriff drops the bags of gold and grabs his sword
from the ground.

ROBIN:            Get ready to die, Sheriff.

*They fight.*

*ROBIN gets the upper hand and then the SHERIFF.*

*Back and forward across the great hall.*

*And then the SHERIFF slips on a gold coin and tumbles to the ground.*

*ROBIN puts his boot on his chest and the point of his sword to his
throat.*

SHERIFF:    Do it! Go on! What are you waiting for?

Robin lifts his sword over his head and is about to attack but then the wolf appears from nowhere and jumps at his throat.

ROBIN:    AAAH!

Robin is knocked to the floor.

Its jaws are locked tight and Robin can feel the life bleeding out of him.

He reaches for his sword.

And stabs the wolf to the heart.

SHERIFF:    What – what did you do?

The Sheriff cradles the body of the wolf.

SHERIFF:    No – no –

ROBIN:    I'm sorry, Sheriff. I – I thought he was going to kill me.

SHERIFF:    My wolf…

ROBIN:    Sheriff, I –

SHERIFF:    Do you see what you've done? You killed him.

ROBIN:    I swear I never meant to –

SHERIFF:    My friend. My brother. He was – he was everything.

The Sheriff looks up at Robin, wet faced and full of despair.

SHERIFF:        I'll go from Nottingham tonight. You will never see me again. I won't take a penny. Is that enough for you?

# 23.

And so Robin turns away from the Sheriff and leaves the great hall and goes into the courtyard.

The soldiers have surrendered.

The castle has fallen.

The people are cheering.

It's over.

Is it?

Yes it's finally over.

What happens next?

Who knows?

Whatever happens next it won't be perfect.

Nothing is, is it?

But it feels like there is a possibility that things will change for the better.

There's hope.

Yes.

Hope at last.

So Robin and his Merry Men gather together, leave the burning ruins of Nottingham Castle and head off back towards the forest.

The sun glows.

And light shines on everything.


*END OF PLAY*

WWW.OBERONBOOKS.COM

Follow us on www.twitter.com/@oberonbooks
& www.facebook.com/OberonBooksLondon